Jum

Allan Ahlberg

Colin McNaughton

Jumping
Dragon's Tail
After Bedtime

RANDOM HOUSE 🏠 NEW YORK

First American Edition, 1986.
Copyright © 1985 by Walker Books Ltd. All rights
reserved under International and Pan-American Copyright
Conventions. Published in the United States by Random
House, Inc., New York. Originally published in Great Britain by
Walker Books Ltd., London.

Library of Congress Cataloging in Publication Data: Ahlberg, Allan. Jumping. (Red nose
readers) Contents: Jumping—Dragon's tail—After bedtime. SUMMARY: Labeled pictures
introduce vocabulary and concepts such as opposites and parts of a whole. 1. Vocabulary—
Juvenile literature. [1. Vocabulary]
I. McNaughton, Colin. · II. Title.   III. Series: Ahlberg, Allan. Red nose readers.
PE1449.A347   1985   428.1   84-27741
ISBN: 0-394-87195-2 (trade); 0-394-97195-7 (lib. bdg.)

Manufactured in Singapore

1 2 3 4 5 6 7 8 9 0

Jumping

jumping

run

running

galloping

gallop

climb

climbing

swing

swinging

diving

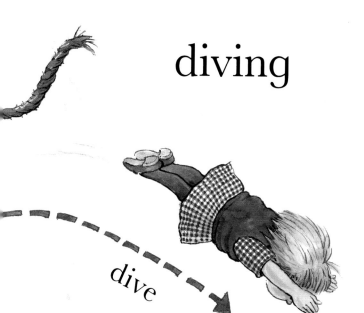

dive

swimming

swim

tunneling

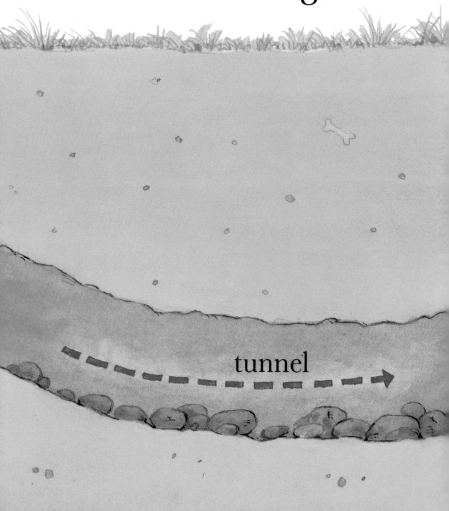

tunnel

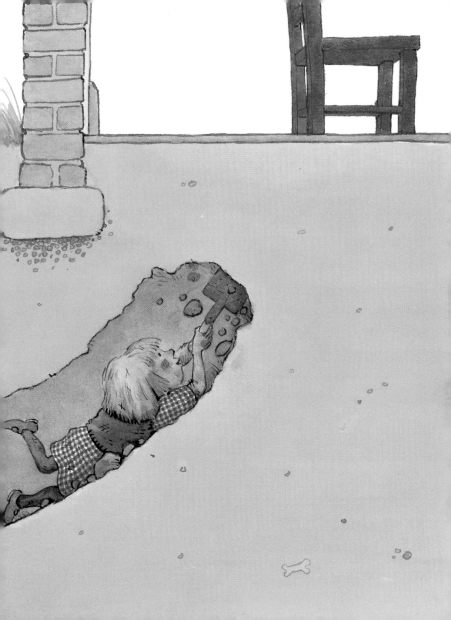

sitting

Dragon's Tail

a horse's head

a dinosaur's body

a crocodile's legs

an elephant's trunk

horse

dinosaur

crocodile

elephant

a bat's wings
a zebra's stripes
a camel's humps
a dragon's tail
make...

bat   zebra

camel   dragon

tail

hump

stripes

body

After Bedtime

before the haircut

after the haircut

before the game

after the game

before the bath

after the bath

before bedtime...

...and after